A 21ST CENTURY SCIENCE, TECHNOLOGY, AND INNOVATION STRATEGY FOR AMERICA'S NATIONAL SECURITY

Committee on Homeland and National Security
OF THE NATIONAL SCIENCE AND TECHNOLOGY COUNCIL

May 2016

Dear Colleagues:

I am pleased to transmit to you "A 21st Century Science, Technology, and Innovation Strategy for America's National Security" (the Strategy). Led by the National Science and Technology Council (NSTC) Committee on Homeland and National Security, in coordination with the Office of Science and Technology Policy, this Strategy reflects input from and deliberation among the science, technology, and innovation components of the Departments and Agencies responsible for carrying out the Nation's national security mission. This Strategy sets forth how the U.S. national security science, technology, and innovation enterprise should evolve to address the challenges and opportunities imposed by a new landscape of national security technology concerns in the 21st century.

The Strategy is informed by the central premise of the President's 2015 National Security Strategy: national security involves much more than military power and homeland defense. The Strategy recognizes that the national security science, technology, and innovation enterprise includes not just the scientists and engineers working in Federal and national laboratories, but also a much larger ecosystem of academic and industry stakeholders. The Strategy acknowledges that the enterprise must continue to drive advances in science, technology, and innovation to assure that the Nation's military and homeland defense remains without peer. But the enterprise also must be able to respond effectively to new challenges, such as asymmetric threats enabled by the globalization of science and technology; threats to stability, such as natural disasters and the effects of climate change; and other humanitarian and security crises, such as epidemic disease.

The Strategy calls for modernization of the enterprise to ensure:
(1)   The ability to access the best talent in the world for the national security mission;
(2)   Proactive and collaborative investments in specialized facilities necessary for critical national security science and technology needs;
(3)   Intelligent management of the business of national security science and technology, and associated risks, to achieve the best outcomes as an enterprise; and
(4)   Adoption of transformative frameworks and innovative practices from the private sector, where it makes sense to do so for the national security mission.

While there is broad agreement on the goals that must be achieved in order to position the enterprise to meet the new challenges and opportunities of the 21st century, there is significant diversity of statutory mission authorities, and structural models and operational authorities, among the many national security agencies that impact how science, technology, and innovation is supported. Therefore, the particular policy and management solutions for achieving these goals may differ significantly among the departments and agencies.

I applaud the work of the NSTC Committee on Homeland and National Security in developing this Strategy, and I ask for their continued diligence in developing and promoting policy and management initiatives that will realize the Strategy's vision for a more agile and resilient national security science, technology, and innovation enterprise.

Sincerely,

John P. Holdren
Assistant to the President for Science and Technology
Director, Office of Science and Technology Policy

About the National Science and Technology Council

The National Science and Technology Council (NSTC) is the principal means by which the Executive Branch coordinates science and technology policy across the diverse entities that make up the Federal research and development (R&D) enterprise. One of the NSTC's primary objectives is establishing clear national goals for Federal science and technology investments. The NSTC prepares R&D packages aimed at accomplishing multiple national goals. The NSTC's work is organized under five committees: Environment, Natural Resources, and Sustainability; Homeland and National Security; Science, Technology, Engineering, and Mathematics (STEM) Education; Science; and Technology. Each of these committees oversees subcommittees and working groups that are focused on different aspects of science and technology. More information is available at www.whitehouse.gov/ostp/nstc.

About the Office of Science and Technology Policy

The Office of Science and Technology Policy (OSTP) was established by the National Science and Technology Policy, Organization, and Priorities Act of 1976. OSTP's responsibilities include advising the President in policy formulation and budget development on questions in which science and technology are important elements; articulating the President's science and technology policy and programs; and fostering strong partnerships among Federal, state, and local governments, and the scientific communities in industry and academia. The Director of OSTP also serves as Assistant to the President for Science and Technology and manages the NSTC. More information is available at www.whitehouse.gov/ostp.

About the Committee on Homeland and National Security

The Committee on Homeland and National Security was established by action of the National Science and Technology Council. Its purpose is to advise and assist the NSTC to increase the overall effectiveness and productivity of Federal research and development efforts in the area of science and technology related to homeland and national security.

About this Document

This document was developed by the Committee on Homeland and National Security. The document was published by OSTP.

Copyright Information

Table of Contents

Introduction

Leadership in science and technology has been the foundation of American national security since World War II. This leadership—coupled with America's capacity for innovation and the ability to translate new ideas into deployable weapons, systems, and concepts of operation—has long ensured the Nation's military advantage.

Our Nation's security relies on more than military advantage, however. The 2015 *National Security Strategy* reaffirms four enduring national interests that guide what America does in the world:[1]

- The security of the United States, its citizens, and U.S. allies and partners;

- A strong, innovative, and growing U.S. economy in an open international economic system that promotes opportunity and prosperity;

- Respect for universal values at home and around the world; and

- A rules-based international order advanced by U.S. leadership that promotes peace, security, and opportunity through stronger cooperation to meet global challenges.

Sustained U.S. leadership in science, technology, and innovation (ST&I) is essential to advancing each of these interests.

A new generation of threats and opportunities has emerged, moreover, which will continue to evolve in unprecedented ways.[2] The United States must continue to lead in developing science and technology solutions to effectively address global problems, such as infectious disease and climate change, which will ultimately affect U.S. national security. The U.S. national security ST&I enterprise must continue to evolve to meet these emerging threats and challenges.

America's national security research and development system is structured to respond to the military threats and economic opportunities of the last century. Recognizing the crucial role of technology in the Second World War, postwar America created an extensive infrastructure for national security science and technology that provided the foundation for the nuclear triad, the intelligence gathering infrastructure, and an array of other military capabilities and advanced tools to meet the threats of the Cold War era. This enterprise nurtured transformative technologies, including stealth technology, integrated command and control, and precision-guided munitions, all designed to counter peer adversaries in large-scale military conflicts.

While such major military missions remain important, the technological implications of emerging threats such as climate change, pandemic disease, cyber-attacks, improvised weapons, and the rise of regional and non-state actors were not anticipated in the design of the current U.S. national security ST&I enterprise. A closed network of national security laboratories and engineering centers and an inwardly-focused national security workforce won the technology races that characterized the Cold War era, but today, the best science and technology is often found outside the national security ST&I enterprise, in academic and commercial sectors in the United States or in other countries. While maintaining military technology overmatch remains a key national security objective, promoting technology development by the private sector at home and around the world and then harnessing that development in ingenious ways will be increasingly important for economic prosperity as well as for national security.

---

[1] http://www.whitehouse.gov/sites/default/files/docs/2015_national_security_strategy_2.pdf.

[2] http://www.dni.gov/files/documents/GlobalTrends_2030.pdf.

In addition, ingrained and sometimes antiquated organizational structures and operational processes pose impediments to the effective use of resources within available budget constraints. These impediments can be overcome by re-imagining the national security ST&I workforce, revitalizing infrastructure, creating new governance approaches and partnerships, and employing innovative tactics to ensure maximum agility, resilience, and efficiency.

This document, *A 21st Century Science, Technology, and Innovation Strategy for America's National Security,* lays out the needs, opportunities, and challenges facing America's national security ST&I enterprise and sets forth a vision for its health and sufficiency enterprise in four critical areas: (1) workforce; (2) facilities and infrastructure; (3) governance roles and responsibilities; and (4) innovative capacity to transform ideas into working technology.

Technology Trends Impacting the National Security ST&I Enterprise

President Obama's 2015 *National Security Strategy* recognizes that military superiority and homeland security are just two dimensions of a set of national security goals that also include ensuring economic prosperity, embracing American values, and providing leadership for the international order. Technological capabilities play a substantial role in all of these aspects of national security. With guidance from the President and Congress, strategic direction and investment priorities for national security science and technology will continue to be determined by Federal mission agencies charged with this responsibility. Those decisions will need to be informed by technology trends described below.

Military

The national security ST&I enterprise must continue to ensure the effectiveness of traditional means of defense and of projecting power, even as the United States prepares for the possibility of new asymmetric and unpredictable threats. Military adversaries possess increasingly more sophisticated and effective weapons that threaten access to shared spaces such as sea, air, space, and the cyber domain. The Nation's capacity to prevail in these domains requires constant monitoring and renewal.

At the same time, the U.S. military is at the cusp of a transformation, with greater use of autonomous and unmanned systems to increase effectiveness and lower costs and personnel risks. Emerging basic and applied research—in areas such as computation and data analytics, engineered materials, nanotechnology, quantum sciences, and cyber-physical systems—is beginning to lay the groundwork for future capabilities that range from hypersonic weapons delivery to highly-secure communications. A number of important areas require increased research effort for security applications, including neuroscience, modeling of human behavior, and synthetic biology.

Affordability will be a driver of future military investments. The costs of technology development can be driven down by applying modeling and simulation tools, leveraging existing commercial innovations and technologies, and using open system architectures, frameworks, and technologies. The coordinated and effective use of prototyping and the intelligent management of risk from basic research through acquisition can also reduce costs, increase capabilities, and maintain technical expertise and organizational agility in the workforce. Shortening the lifecycle of capability development can allow more effective response to emerging needs, provide additional technology-development experience for the workforce, enable a higher cadence of technology refreshment, and promote industrial innovation. Technology can also be used to make basic and operational training more effective and efficient, as well as to augment human cognitive and physical performance.

Homeland Security

Technology can provide solutions to maintain homeland security while protecting civil liberties and facilitating the legal flow of people, goods, and services across U.S. borders. Development of better data integration, predictive modeling, and risk-analysis capabilities will provide prompt, actionable information to decision makers. In addition, detecting and addressing threats as early and as far away as possible requires that the United States apply technological solutions in cooperation with tourism, trade, and security partners. The Nation must continue to invest in advanced cybersecurity protection and training, both to protect critical infrastructure from cyber threats and promote the understanding that cybersecurity is the responsibility of all sectors of society.

Intelligence

Diplomatic, military, and homeland security operations are supported by robust intelligence capabilities. The United States must invest heavily in the science and technology of tools for intelligence to increase U.S. capabilities for collecting security-relevant information around the world and leverage intelligence integration to provide a global intelligence advantage. National security will increasingly be affected by global trends and fast-moving emerging and disruptive developments in science, technology, and innovation capacity. The intelligence community must continue to build the partnership activities that are linking the ST&I community to collectors, analysts, and decision makers so as to ensure that key intelligence capabilities are robust and available to achieve national security objectives.

Manufacturing

The Nation's security depends on a healthy manufacturing sector, which in turn requires trusted, secure, and adequate supply chains, and resilient and affordable critical infrastructure such as electric power, natural gas, communications, and transportation systems. Cutting-edge national security technology needs historically have provided initial manufacturing demand for the later development of robust commercial markets that contribute to national security through economic strength. The national security ST&I enterprise, including the government, academic, and industry components, must do its part in ensuring that the United States maintains a healthy manufacturing sector. The enterprise should anticipate and be prepared to support the development of manufacturing expertise in fast moving areas of emerging and disruptive technology that are relevant to national security, including additive manufacturing, nanotechnology, bio-materials, flexible microelectronics, and other areas.

Advanced Computing and Communications

The exponential growth of the digital economy, driven by ubiquitous computing and communication technologies, holds tremendous potential for innovation, economic competitiveness, and national security. New and rapidly evolving technological capabilities such as high-performance computing, next-generation networks, and the Internet of Things will change the ways that data are created, analyzed, and disseminated across a wide spectrum of uses. The Federal Government will build on foundational technologies, such as big-data analytics and the improved collection and sharing of data, to provide managers and policy makers with the tools they need to make timely and effective decisions. The Federal Government will continue to foster policies for addressing data ownership, access, and control—as well as spectrum management—in ways that balance privacy protection, cybersecurity, national security, and economic interests.

Resilient, Clean, and Affordable Energy

Improving domestic energy security and supply, reducing the environmental impacts of energy use, and improving reliability and resilience of energy systems are necessary to maintaining America's National Security at home. Developing new technologies to reduce or eliminate the energy supply chain for our deployed military can save resources and improve the operational capability of our armed forces. Sharing technology for energy security with developing nations can reduce global instability. Addressing these challenges will require sustained investment in technology research and development and may be enhanced by encouraging market pull for advanced energy systems.

Challenges and Opportunities for the National Security ST&I Enterprise

The structure and function of the national security ST&I enterprise need to address not only the global landscape as it exists today, but also the drivers that are reshaping that landscape. The enterprise is facing the following external and internal challenges and opportunities.

Globalization of Science and Technology

Worldwide, investment in scientific research and development is increasing at a faster pace than it is in the United States. Although the European Union, Japan, and North America still account for the majority of global science and technology investment, relative shares are shifting due to substantial growth in several Asian economies.[3] This global investment is accompanied by rapid growth of ST&I talent in the rest of the world, accelerated by the increasing internationalization of the scientific research enterprise and the global flow of knowledge. The United States is no longer assured of leadership in all areas of science and technology critical to national security.

Dramatically increased capacity for science and technology around the world provides not only increased challenges but also increased opportunities to collaborate with partners around the world in the development of technology for U.S. and global security. The goodwill that the United States has generated from ST&I diplomacy and international development is a key enabler for global cooperation, and the enterprise must continue to build and strengthen such relationships.

Asymmetric and Unpredictable Threats

Threats to national security are often asymmetric, with human or economic risks to the United States far greater than the resources required to develop and deploy the threats. Threats are often difficult to predict because modern science and technology enable many opportunities to cause harm; significant scientific knowledge is instantly available worldwide; and threats do not necessarily require an established scientific or industrial infrastructure that the United States can monitor. The global proliferation of the cyber domain imposes risks to cyber infrastructure and creates the unwanted possibility of instant widespread dissemination of national-security-sensitive information.

While advances in many areas of technology are not being driven by weapons production or weapons-focused R&D, many of the capabilities being developed have significant dual-use potential. Digital connectivity, for instance, brings tremendous societal and economic benefits, enabling rapid flow of information to all corners of the globe. The convergence of engineering design, mathematical analysis, and molecular biology presents opportunities to create entirely novel processes and capabilities in living organisms on a much more rapid scale than traditional recombinant DNA techniques, and to share these designs digitally. Nanotechnology promises the ability to engineer entirely new high-performance materials. Additive manufacturing (3-D printing) will dramatically shrink the barriers between design concepts and reality. These and many other domains of science and technology promise extraordinary

---

[3] National Science Board, *Science and Engineering Indicators 2016*, 2016. http://www.nsf.gov/statistics/2016/nsb20161/

economic and social gains for our Nation and the world, but all can potentially be put to use for destructive purposes.

Natural Disasters and Humanitarian Crises

Threats to global stability posed by challenges such as pandemics, extreme poverty and resource scarcity, climate change, and natural disasters require proactive and collaborative solutions that are enabled by scientific and technological advances. The increasing mobility of people and goods across national borders increases the importance and vulnerability of the global commons and escalates the risks posed by threats from infectious diseases. Pressures exerted on natural resources and the climate by expanding global populations and increased demand from a growing middle class have political and socio-economic impacts that threaten global stability and supply chains that support national security.

The United States plays a vital role in mitigating humanitarian crises and in promoting global stability. The Administration recognizes that few global problems can be solved without U.S. action but also that few can be solved by the United States alone. Whether by developing technologies to deploy around the world for humanitarian purposes or participating in ST&I diplomacy to build global capacity, the national security ST&I enterprise must learn to adopt an integrated approach that leverages strengths and capabilities wherever they exist.

Inversion of Technology Flow

Advances such as radar and global positioning navigation were developed by the national security ST&I enterprise, and these technologies found broader application later when they became available to the private sector. Today, private-sector commercial technology advances often outpace developments within the Federal national security mission agencies. There is an opportunity for the national security system to benefit from the investments of the private sector and leverage the best technology advances. The national security ST&I enterprise is not currently equipped with tools and processes to identify the best commercial technologies and apply them to national security problems in a timely way. While frameworks and mechanisms exist in specialized cases for harnessing private-sector innovation, too often the most agile and innovative companies are unwilling to work with government national security customers due to the time, cost, and complexity imposed by Federal acquisition processes.

Offshoring of Technological Capacity

As multinational corporations take advantage of the globalization of technology development capabilities and changing economic environments, their priorities may compete with or overshadow national security interests. This has significant national security implications, as domestic commercial companies strive to maintain their competitive edge by offshoring their manufacturing operations, many of which are part of the supply chains of national-security-critical technologies. Domestic companies also have been steadily increasing investments in their offshore research facilities to leverage the economic and collaborative benefits of globalization. Critical research and development advances are taking place outside the purview of the U.S. national security ST&I enterprise, and the United States could lose leadership in entire areas of domestic technology capacity.

Aging National Security ST&I Infrastructure

The remarkable achievements of the national security ST&I enterprise in the decades after the Second World War were enabled by investments made over decades in special and unique—and now aging— facilities and infrastructure. Many of these physical plants date to the dawn of the Cold War or even before, and reinvestment in many cases has been on hold due to other priorities. The race to stay ahead of the increasingly sophisticated technology of potential adversaries—and enable continuing support of partners and allies—requires continued and responsive investment in cutting-edge scientific and engineering facilities, platform technologies, information technology, equipment, and instrumentation.

Recognizing the realities of budget constraints, the ST&I enterprise has an opportunity to do better than simply rebuilding or expanding existing physical infrastructure. While security issues must be carefully managed, the enterprise now has the opportunity to reconsider the concept of the walls and fences around facilities. Can the enterprise protect what needs to be protected while cooperating effectively with universities and industry? Can the enterprise build the sorts of physical and cyber infrastructure that promote scientific and technical collaboration, promote meaningful technology transfer for the creation of economic value, and allow entrepreneurs and industry to share facilities, equipment, and production capacity? In some cases, efforts similar to the Army Research Laboratory's Open Campus Initiative or the Department of Homeland Security's National Bio and Agro-Defense Facility might serve to increase the effectiveness of U.S. national security ST&I facilities by co-locating and integrating academia, industry, and traditional defense laboratories.

Challenges for the National Security ST&I Workforce

The recruitment and development of a generation of talented scientists and engineers who dedicated their careers to national security was critical to the Cold War technology achievements of the United States. The national security technical workforce flourished in part because the mission was important and the government enterprise provided the best opportunity to do high-quality and cutting-edge technical work. Over time, less-positive perceptions of service in the Federal Government and declining Federal research budgets have threatened the Federal Government's ability to attract and retain ST&I talent in key areas of national security capability. Ensuring a diverse and inclusive workplace environment to support a culture of innovation in the national security ST&I enterprise remains a significant challenge.

Science and engineering are based on intellectual exchange and collaboration, and groundbreaking technical work requires close-knit and nurtured teams of talented individuals with the freedom to explore and grow. If the U.S. national security ST&I workforce is not valued or treated well, the enterprise risks jeopardizing the call to service and tradition of excellence. Rules meant to promote the responsible use of resources have had unintended consequences. For example, restrictions on travel and conference attendance have diminished the ability of Federal scientists and engineers to advance their technical skills and take advantage of opportunities for technical exchange with the wider professional science and engineering community. The best and brightest scientists and engineers have many opportunities in today's technology-rich world, and the national security ST&I enterprise must be able to attract and access this talent and provide the tools, processes, and working environment that will sustain motivation and excellence.

The Federal Government maintains cumbersome human-resources barriers compared to the best private-sector and university practices. Unlike previous generations, the majority of workers of today and tomorrow may embark on career journeys that are not tied to a single institution with the expectation of lifetime employment. An ability to embrace the healthy and sustainable flow among sectors and organizations that is characteristic of modern private-sector technical careers would improve the quality, flow, and diversity of new entrants in the workforce for national security ST&I.

While the call for public service and the national security mission are important in attracting technical talent into Federal service, Federal Government salaries generally are not competitive with other technology employers. In particular, government compensation lags significantly at senior levels, making lateral recruitment from other sectors of qualified and experienced leadership and management talent extremely challenging. With a few exceptions, current regulations and statutory limitations make it very difficult to arrange for exchange or rotational experiences with the private and academic sectors.

Opportunities to Revitalize the National Security ST&I Workforce

By some estimates, almost half of current national security scientists and engineers will become eligible to retire within the coming decade.[4] Ensuring a robust pipeline of qualified science, technology, engineering, and mathematics (STEM) talent remains problematic, including the ability to recruit from a diverse pool of American citizens eligible for the clearances necessary for national security work[5]. While U.S. citizenship will continue to be required for those working in sensitive areas, the institutions that contribute to the national security science, technology, and innovation infrastructure should be, wherever possible, able to draw on the world's best and brightest minds regardless of citizenship. The coming wave of retirements affords a once-in-a-generation opportunity for the Federal Government to fundamentally rethink personnel policies to sustain, cultivate, reshape, and promote a world-class national security ST&I workforce. Reliable support for evidence-based programs designed to maintain a diverse and robust STEM education pipeline, including providing robust STEM opportunities for the children of military families at home and abroad, is critical for the U.S. national security ST&I workforce.

Opportunities in Science, Technology, and Innovation Diplomacy

American values of democracy, rule of law, and freedom of expression help to guide collaboration and norms for conduct in the international scientific community. American scientists and engineers promote meritocracy, transparency, open data, sharing of scientific information and ideas, reproducibility of scientific results, critical thinking, diversity of thought, and respect for intellectual property. International engagement and the formation of partnerships in ST&I provide a platform to share these values, create linkages among international science communities, promote greater participation of women and underrepresented minorities in science and engineering, and highlight the role of civil society and non-governmental actors.

Science and technology support governments in formulating evidence-based policies, meeting challenges, and combating threats to international order, including climate change; natural disasters; wildlife trafficking; water, food, and energy security; polar issues; ocean conservation; pandemics; and space security. The United States is committed to harnessing technology and making data available to mitigate the impact of disasters through open mapping, open data, crowdsourced solutions, and other means. Promoting access to high-quality STEM education, training, and opportunities will be a part of U.S. ST&I outreach around the world.

ST&I for Global Development and Stability

International development and capacity building efforts for ST&I will help strengthen the global innovation community, expand access to the Internet and communications technologies, create economic opportunities, reduce the risk of conflict, and promote human rights. ST&I are tools for the growth of democracy around the world, and the national security ST&I enterprise will continue to facilitate access to information, freedom of expression, and the coordination of democratic groups.

---

[4] Department of Defense Laboratory Civilian Science and Engineering Workforce 2013. Defense Laboratories Office, Office of the Assistant Secretary of Defense (Research and Engineering)

[5] Federal Science, Technology, Engineering, and Mathematics (STEM) Education 5-Year Strategic Plan (2013). A report from the National Science and Technology Council Committee on STEM Education.

ST&I can also play a critical role in advancing the Federal Government's global-development objectives and thereby strengthen national security. The United States is in a unique position to help lead efforts to resolve one of humanity's most entrenched and difficult challenges by the year 2030: persistent extreme poverty.[6] This aim can be achieved through a new model of development grounded in evidence-based evaluation, rapid iteration, country ownership, sustainability, and strategic public- and private-sector partnerships that catalyze talent and innovation everywhere.

Digital infrastructure is the new foundation of the 21st century economy. Like roads, railways, and the power grid, digital technologies have transformed markets and unleashed innovation by creating platforms for new ideas, new business models, and new modes of communication and collaboration. Increased digital infrastructure access and inclusion around the world have been and must remain a priority for U.S. efforts in global development.

The enterprise should also invest in science and technology aimed at understanding behavior and culture around the world. Modeling and analytical tools that fuse information-based trend analysis with socio-cultural-behavioral awareness can lead to a better understanding of steps that can be taken to mitigate potential risks before they become crises. Technology can also help to combat decentralized criminal threats, such as the trafficking of people and drugs.

Policy Solutions for an Agile and Resilient National Security ST&I Enterprise

An agile and resilient national security ST&I enterprise can balance openness to the global science and technology community with the protection of technological advantage needed to ensure the security of the Nation and its allies. The enterprise must accept and manage technological risk related to new technologies while ensuring the security and stewardship of critical existing capabilities. It must understand and support the promise of technological convergence while preserving technical domain expertise of the highest caliber. Basic and applied research and prototyping functions can be efficiently distributed to national security and academic laboratories and industrial development centers. Costs can be reduced and flexibility can be increased without sacrificing quality. Continuous evolution of the enterprise can ensure sustained agility and resilience as new threats and challenges present themselves in the future.

Achieving this vision will require targeted strategic coordination and investment in four key areas of the national ST&I enterprise: (1) workforce, (2) facilities and infrastructure, (3) governance roles and responsibilities, and (4) innovative capacity to transform ideas into working technology. Already, Federal departments and agencies have worked on model policies and pilot programs in each of these areas.

Quality, Flow, and Diversity of the National Security ST&I Workforce

The national security ST&I enterprise is responsible for hiring the scientists and engineers that will sustain its critical mission. To solve the toughest national security challenges, the United States must grow STEM capacity by strengthening the STEM engagement, teaching, mentoring, and training pipeline, then attract the best and brightest STEM talent to the national security sector, and continue to retain access to that talent throughout the course of a modern technical career.

Developing STEM talent for national security. The national security mission agencies must continue to partner with other STEM agencies to ensure a pipeline of qualified talent. The national security mission

---

[6] Transforming our World: The 2030 Agenda for Sustainable Development. The United Nations, 2015.

agencies have a number of roles to play as partners with other STEM agencies: (1) maintaining a detailed understanding of their own STEM workforce needs and investing where necessary to ensure an adequate supply, particularly in the critical technical areas where training might not be assured by the needs of the larger labor market; (2) communicating to young people the opportunities available in the national security ST&I enterprise and the special requirements that exist for being a part of the national security community; (3) embracing the use of laddering opportunities, such as high school and college internships, scholarship for service, fellowships, and other means of attracting quality talent; and (4) committing, particularly at the early career development stages, to making training opportunities and national security STEM career awareness outreach available to all, including women, underrepresented minorities, and people with disabilities. Healthy STEM outreach programs by laboratory scientists and engineers are a valuable means to build community relations, maintain employee morale, and impact broad STEM education and national security STEM workforce efforts.

Attracting, recruiting, and hiring STEM talent. National security ST&I workforce needs can be assessed on a whole-of-government basis, based on skills rather than occupations, and within the context of a more competitive private-sector and global marketplace. Agencies must continue to expand the range of tools available to attract technical and management talent in a competitive market, including developing a common branding to market the national security enterprise. The mechanisms by which the national security technical workforce is recruited, shaped, and retained must be modernized. Strong connections between the national security ST&I workforce and the agency missions must be articulated and valued by agency leadership. To strengthen the national security ST&I workforce, the enterprise must be empowered and encouraged by Federal department and agency leadership to make faster hiring decisions and experiment with flexible personnel approaches and authorities. Federal science and technology organizations must train and encourage their human capital teams and leadership to exchange successful technical-workforce planning practices and effectively utilize these existing authorities to improve the recruitment and retention of qualified talent, including with respect to underrepresented populations in STEM. Sensible immigration policies, including for skilled immigrants in specialty technical areas, particularly for those educated in U.S. universities, must continue to be a goal.

Promoting cross-sector flow to retain access to STEM talent. The modern technical career comprises a variety of work experiences, often in multiple organizations. Agility and resilience in the national security ST&I enterprise may best be served by promoting the robust flow of talent between the public, private, and academic sectors. Expanded use of the Intergovernmental Personnel Act (IPA), topical reserve corps, and other mechanisms can permit cross-sector flow through personnel exchanges. Broader training and professional development opportunities can promote collaboration and idea exchange. Increasing the exposure of policymakers to technical experts and research results, both inside and outside of government, can enable the Federal Government to more effectively create well-informed, evidence-based policy in the face of rapidly advancing technology. Laws that address employee and institutional conflicts of interest should be updated to manage risks intelligently and flexibly. Security clearances and associated processes should be managed to promote flow of credentialed talent between the sectors.

Facilitating knowledge exchange. Collaborative thought and the exchange of ideas are the basis of science and technology advances. Departments and agencies will foster a continuous learning environment so that Federal national security scientists and engineers can easily access the full range of professional opportunities for interaction that are offered to the broader science and technology community, including, as appropriate, participation in scientific conferences and workshops, and service in the leadership of scientific and technical societies and other professional organizations. Federal scientists and engineers must be afforded the opportunity to explore entrepreneurial opportunities and earn rewards and incentives based on their work products.

Modern Infrastructure that Promotes Excellence and Collaboration

Modern scientific infrastructure is needed to explore complex topics, gather data for computational models, and test hypotheses in the pursuit of scientific discovery. State-of-the-art science and technology facilities, platform technologies, information technology, equipment, and instrumentation maximize opportunities for hands-on engagement, discovery, and practical application, promoting invention and innovation and speeding the scaling and commercial development of new ideas. America's national security ST&I enterprise maintains a diverse array of special equipment and facilities that are often unique in the world. While existing facilities and infrastructure offer a range of niche and complementary capabilities, some are approaching the end of their useful life or are in serious need of modernization.

Effective strategic planning for ST&I infrastructure. Rather than responding to infrastructure crises as they occur, the enterprise must more consistently build and execute a strategic approach for renewal of existing facilities and for development of new facilities that will be needed in the future. Where multiple agencies depend on shared ST&I facilities, it is critical that effective arrangements for cooperative planning and management be in place.

Technical workplaces worthy of the best talent. While the enterprise can and must be good stewards of taxpayer resources, working environment and available tools directly affect the quality of the work performed by ST&I talent. The infrastructure investments of the best private firms reflect their understanding that purposeful architecture and well-maintained surroundings have a significant impact on the creativity and motivation of a specialized technical workforce. The national security ST&I enterprise should be enabled to recruit cutting-edge scientists and engineers and provide them with workplace information, communication, and collaboration technologies that are not older and more cumbersome than what they may have in their own homes.

Sharing specialized facilities across sectors. To revitalize the Nation's aging research and development infrastructure, creative policies are needed that will enable the Federal Government to share specialized facilities with the public and private sectors as capacity permits, and use updated financial mechanisms to increase the affordability of facility revitalization and construction. Where it is not critical to build and maintain specialized ST&I facilities for the sole purpose of national security, collaboration with the Nation's wider ST&I community will be encouraged and supported through open campus arrangements and the promotion of robust ecosystems for collaboration with academia and the private sector.

Agile and Effective Governance

Governance policies and practices used to manage science and technology procurement and performance must be modernized and streamlined to best serve national security ST&I needs in a changing global environment. These policies and practices will enable agile technology investment, enhance mission clarity and research strategy, ensure appropriate levels of oversight and compliance with regulatory standards, and facilitate full-spectrum use of available funding mechanisms and collaborations.

Full and proactive use of granted authorities. To the extent possible, management should be decentralized and decisions should be pushed to the local level, including management of the workforce according to budget as opposed to fixed personnel limits. Agencies should encourage field activities to take the fullest advantage of agile personnel and innovative contracting authorities that have been granted by Congress. The national security ST&I enterprise, in collaboration with Congress and the Administration, must continue to improve governance and business practices through ongoing, common-sense adjustments rather than responding to crises after the fact.

An inclusive concept of the national security ST&I enterprise. Frameworks for improved engagement and strategic planning for coordination among the various stakeholders in the national security ST&I

enterprise—academic institutions; nonprofit corporations; small and large private-sector firms; Federal laboratories, centers, and agencies; and multilateral standard-setting organizations—will greatly enhance the quality and speed of research and development. Rules and regulations must be streamlined in order to enhance the flexibility of national security agencies to partner with academic and private stakeholders and to take advantage of best practices across sectors. The enterprise must support removing barriers where possible to encourage the participation of innovative stakeholders that may not work with the enterprise today, and bring to bear the abilities of the performers best positioned to meet national security mission needs. In particular, the enterprise must leverage the commercial sector's ability to rapidly develop technologies that can meet national security needs by offering small businesses greater and more cost-effective access to Federal laboratories and special facilities where excess capacity exists.

Open Approaches to Innovation

Embracing principled and robust use of modern innovation tools for problem-solving and acquisition, and making the fruits of the national security ST&I enterprise available for entrepreneurial efforts, can result in better solutions for national security problems, a more engaged, connected, and outward-looking workforce, and economic benefits.

Opening the aperture of innovation. Some of the best ST&I capacity and ideas will be found outside of the national security enterprise and indeed outside of the United States. Careful attention also must be paid by both the enterprise and the intelligence community to ST&I developments worldwide. While the U.S. Government engages in ST&I diplomacy across the whole of government, many national security science and technology departments and agencies have unique authorities to provide resources and to enter into partnerships internationally. The results and relationships deriving from international ST&I work must be better integrated across the Federal Government.

Innovative and agile granting and contracting. Innovative approaches to acquisition and intellectual property create opportunities for U.S. entrepreneurs and companies while furthering the mission of the enterprise. Non-traditional granting and contracting mechanisms—such as Other Transactions Authority, incentive prizes, advance market commitments, challenge-based acquisition, and agile approaches to software development and information system procurement—increase the speed, quality, diversity, and number of performers contributing to government missions.[7]

Accelerating transitions from lab to market. The cost, time, and risk to develop and commercialize innovative technologies may prohibit market-driven development of new tools and technologies in areas of critical importance to national security. The enterprise must ensure that taxpayers can benefit from Federally-funded research and development by maintaining timely, effective, and coordinated intellectual property and technology transition programs that provide incentives for innovation and the development of technology. The transition of the results of Federally-funded research and development from laboratory to market can be accelerated by enhancing successful programs, such as the Small Business Innovative Research and Small Business Technology Transfer programs, and by promoting government-sponsored venture capital funds, such as those pioneered by the intelligence community.

---

[7] See *Innovative Contracting Case Studies*, Office of Science and Technology and the Office of Federal Procurement Policy, available at http://www.whitehouse.gov/blog/2014/08/21/buying-what-works-case-studies-innovative-contracting-0

Conclusion

The elements of a secure Nation articulated by the *2015 National Security Strategy* encompass the multiple aspirations of security, prosperity, global values, and international order. Science, technology, and innovation contribute to all of these dimensions of national security. The national security ST&I enterprise must be able to meet rapidly evolving threats, establish and maintain strategic partnerships, employ swiftly changing technologies, cope with diminishing resources, and benefit from accelerating globalization.

The U.S. national security ST&I enterprise derives its strength from mission agencies, in collaboration with academia, industry, and global partners. Recognizing the new realities of a globally-interconnected, fast-evolving science and technology landscape that presents new threats and opportunities, the policy directions called for in this strategy present a vision for a vibrant national security ST&I enterprise for the 21st century that is agile, resilient, and capable of delivering technological advantages to the United States. To ensure sustained U.S. leadership, the foundational capabilities that span all agencies and departments of the national security enterprise—diverse human capital, quality infrastructure, modern management systems, multi-sector partnerships, and strong research programs—must be strengthened and revitalized.

Abbreviations

NSTC	National Science and Technology Council
OSTP	Office of Science and Technology Policy
R&D	research and development
STEM	Science, Technology, Engineering, and Mathematics
ST&I	Science, Technology, & Innovation
IPA	Intergovernmental Personnel Act